POSITIVE AFFIRMATIONS FOR TEENAGE GIRLS

POSITIVE AFFIRMATIONS FOR TEENAGE GIRLS

Beat Stress, Think Positive and Grow Stronger in 50 Days

Lucy Wynn

Book Design and Typesetting by Irissa Book Design
on LinkedIn and Facebook

Bonus Book

Want to get this book for free?

You can receive it by email for FREE and for an unlimited time by joining our community below.

Contents

Week 3: Gratitude 37

Week 4: Anxiety and Stress 53

Week 5: Happiness 69

Week 6: Success 85

Week 7: The Future 101

My Diary
Today was a great day

Introduction

When I was a preteen and teenager, I was the shy kid who used to sit at the back of the class, avoiding all the questions the teacher would ask. I felt insecure about myself, scared that if I spoke up, the other kids would laugh and tell me I was wrong. Even the possibility of making mistakes on homework and doing badly on tests made me worry. I also wasn't comfortable in my skin and didn't like to grab anyone's attention. I felt like people judged me and my choice of school clothes; constantly feeling self-conscious about it.

Growing up is hard. The more you find out about the world and yourself, the harder it is to make sense of it. You feel like your parents don't understand and good friends are hard to find. There's this overwhelming sense of pressure coming from all different sides of your life. When you become a teenager, people expect you to know what you want to do in the future when you can't even remember what you ate for dinner last night. It can be a very stressful time. I understand how difficult it can be since I struggled with my mental health throughout my teenage years.

Negative thoughts constantly popped up in my head and I didn't know what to do about them. I didn't understand why I was so depressed the whole time or why I didn't enjoy life. It was difficult to realize that, in your teenage years, it's normal to go through big changes in mood throughout your day and to feel negative and judged.

I only realized later that there are things you can do to change those negative thoughts to become happier. When I was older, I discovered the amazing power of positive affirmations and journaling, but wished I had found them earlier! No one was there to tell me how to handle my negative emotions, and because of this, growing up was very hard for me.

Now, helping others and encouraging them to achieve great things is what I love to do. I love to support others going through a difficult time while helping them understand that there are things you can do about it. I would love to assist you on your journey of discovering yourself. I'm here to help you change your mindset into something positive and uplifting!

This book is to encourage young girls to discover the power of journaling and positive affirmations. But most importantly, it is to encourage girls to remember to have fun! I want to show them that this is still possible, even though they are growing up.

To use this book, follow along and read a page a day. There are 50 days divided into seven weeks for you to explore! Each week deals with a different, useful topic for you to think and learn about. Every page also has a positive paragraph filled with affirmations and tips, followed by some reflection points and a short, simple task for you to do. After 50 days, you'll have all the tools needed to navigate mentally through the challenges of your teenage years.

For each day, lightly write your ideas and thoughts in pencil on the blocks provided. This will make it easy to erase the things you've written and write something new!

However, don't feel pressured to write things down or do these tasks. Do whatever makes you feel comfortable. This book is for you and you alone. You can choose what you would like to do with it. By the end, if I've made you smile or think about something even once, then I've reached my goal.

Week 1
Self-Love

Day 1

What is Self-Love?

The first step to self-love is recognizing what it is. Self-love simply means to love and accept yourself for who you are. To spend time with yourself and make sure you love and treat yourself properly.

It's never a waste of time to spend some time with yourself!

In this world, where there are millions of things happening, it can be difficult to realize this is necessary to do.

Think of the stars. There are millions of stars and you don't see every single one, but you notice the brightest ones. I'd like to think that the ones that shine the brightest are the happiest, most radiant and most confident ones. And the only way to get yourself to shine brightly is to be happy with who you are. Self-love is the first step towards being that bright star in the sky. Part of the self-love journey is accepting yourself fully. You were created to be unique and to stand out.

Thought Bubble

- *Have you thought about yourself today?*
- *How are you feeling?*

Write down the following to start thinking about self-love.

- *What are five things you like about yourself?*

I want to challenge you today. Say the things you like about yourself out loud. Forget about what you don't like for now. If you have a negative thought, list the things you like about yourself in your head.

Day 2

Make Mistakes

Part of self-love is accepting yourself for who you are. The whole you. Not just a tiny part, but everything about you. Even the time you fell in front of your crush, or when you said something stupid, or when you laughed at something you shouldn't have. Accept all your mistakes and failures and forgive yourself for them.

It's a part of life and a part of who you are. And the good thing is, everyone makes mistakes. No one is perfect. Even though someone seems perfect, they aren't. That is the one thing we all have in common. Because we were made to make mistakes and learn from them. It's never a bad thing to laugh at your own mistakes. This makes these mistakes more light-hearted and not as serious. We weren't made to be perfect. Imagine how boring that would be!

If you think about mistakes as something positive, you will let go of your mistakes quicker. Think of it as a paper you have to throw away. If you keep the crumpled up paper on your desk, you will think about the paper the whole time. But if you throw it away, you can move on and start out fresh on a new piece.

When you accept your mistakes, you can move past them quicker.

Thought Bubble

- Write down any mistakes you've made that have been bothering you on a separate piece of paper.
- Now, take this list of mistakes, crumple up the paper it's on, and throw it away. You can even rip it up into pieces if that makes you feel good.
- Then, think of a mistake you made and write it down in a funny way. Make fun of this mistake. In that way, you can let go of it easier.

Day 3

Be Kind

Our harshest critics are often ourselves. To love yourself fully, you need to stop judging yourself as harshly as you do. We are often overly critical of ourselves because we know what we are capable of. We see ourselves from a zoomed-in perspective.

So, for example, think of a picture you look at on a phone. Now imagine zooming in as close as you can. Of course, the picture won't look good because you're looking at the tiniest details that people don't even notice. That's what we do with ourselves. We pick apart every funny looking freckle, every little hair out of place, and every small thing. You are a full picture, not a zoomed-in one.

We are too harsh on ourselves because we can't see ourselves from another perspective. You might think: *I have this big, ugly pimple on my nose that everyone will see. What are they going to think of me?* While no one even notices.

But you have to keep in mind that being this judgmental and critical of yourself will not help you move forward. You will often feel worse than you already do when you pick apart every tiny thing.

Being kind to yourself is a hard thing to do, but it's one of the best things you can do for you.

Thought Bubble

- Can you think of an example in your life where you've been very harsh on yourself?
- Go stand in front of the mirror and zoom in on one thing that bothers you.
- Now walk away from the mirror and notice that this tiny detail becomes invisible when you look at yourself as a whole.

Day 4

Me Time

If you don't feel you love yourself or take care of yourself, it's time for "me time." You never waste time when you spend it on yourself. Even if it feels like you are being unproductive or like there are a million other things you can do, spending time with yourself is so important.

It's easy to forget to just breathe and relax when you're having a busy day. That's why we need some time to get to know ourselves again. Imagine bumping into yourself while walking home. What would you ask when trying to check up on you? Maybe things like, "How are you feeling? How has your day been?"

"Me time" is all about spending quality time with yourself. Just like you would do with friends and family, to catch up on what's been going on in their lives.

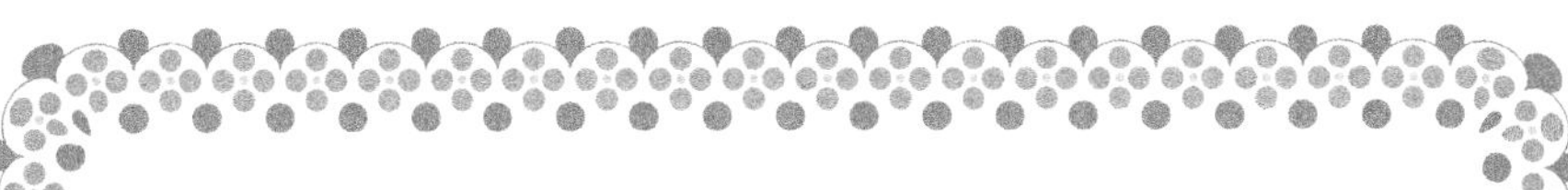

Thought Bubble

- Spend at least a few minutes on your own just relaxing and thinking about your day.
- Think about how you feel, what you have done, what has been good in your day, what has been bad, and what tomorrow brings.
- Write these thoughts in a journal and discover how you're feeling while you write.

Day 5

Be Yourself

In a world where there are so many people around, it's easy to blend in with the crowd. But you were made to stand out! If we weren't, every single person would have looked the same and done the same things.

So let's celebrate our differences. It's okay to be different from others. It's okay to stand out and be yourself fully. And it's okay to love yourself for it. Don't let anyone tell you you're not allowed to be who you are. Who gives them the right to tell you that? You live with yourself and you have to love yourself. If you can't be yourself, you will feel negative, sad, and depressed.

When you are free to be yourself, you can express yourself fully and be happy. Our uniqueness makes us interesting human beings. People want to find out who you are as a person because of how you are. And yes, some people might not like you for being yourself, but those people don't matter. What matters is that you like yourself. If you like you, others will like you too. Even if it's just one person, there will always be someone who likes you for you.

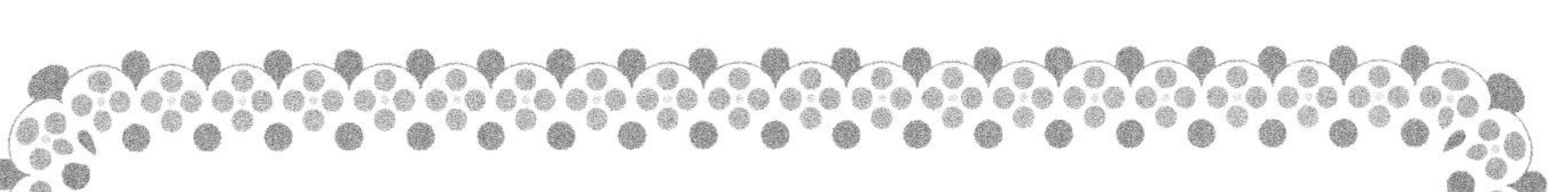

Thought Bubble

- List a few things that you think are unique about you.
- Write how you think you can celebrate this uniqueness.

Day 6

Have Fun

In our busy lives filled with schoolwork, daily house tasks, and more, we forget to have fun every once in a while. It's okay to let loose and to enjoy life. Go jump in a jumping castle, watch funny videos on YouTube, play your favorite music, and dance like no one's watching. Or, have a sleepover with friends and watch the movies you love. Just because you're getting older doesn't mean you can't have any fun.

Forget about what everyone thinks. Do what you want to do. It isn't good to stress and worry all day. By having fun, you're practicing self-love and taking a break from everything stressful in life.

Be sure to be a kid now and then. Use your imagination and be creative. Do something you've always wanted to do.

Thought Bubble

- Think of one thing you enjoyed doing as a kid.
- Think of something you can do now that you will enjoy.
- Don't be afraid to have fun and do the things you have written. Life doesn't have to be dull and gloomy.

Day 7

Self-Care

If you love something, you take care of it, don't you? Now, this is exactly what you should do with yourself as well. Taking care of yourself will help you spend time with and love yourself more. Here are a few things you can do to start taking care of yourself.

Eating the right amount of food for your body is important. When people stress, they tend to either eat too little or too much. Even if you feel like there isn't enough time in your day to eat, you always have to make time for food. Listen to what your body is telling you.

To feel good, you also have to look good. Taking care of little things, like hygiene, will help you feel good when you walk out the door for school. Take care of your skin, hair, nails, and anything else you feel is important.

Often when you feel down, exercising can be a good way to re-energize your mind. Exercising will get you into a positive and motivated mindset.

Whenever you feel down, think of something you can do to take care of yourself and do it.

Thought Bubble

- Ask yourself the following questions: When was the last time I ate? Am I hungry? Am I thirsty?
- Think of self-care things you can do that will make you feel good. For example: having a bubble bath, painting your nails, spending time picking out a nice outfit.
- Now, do at least one of these things each day.

Week 2
Friendship and Family

Day 8

What Friends and Family Do

It's a new week. And with it, we welcome a new theme.

People are an interesting species. We struggle to live without each other. Imagine waking up in the middle of a field with no one around. There are no houses, no transportation, and there is no way of getting home. You have nothing with you. What would you do?

I would probably panic. Even if we think we can live without other people, we really can't. We might live without them for a few weeks, and if you're really pushing it, for a few months. But by then, you would crave any conversation you can get. The birds might be good at conversations; you never know. That's why we need the support of others around us. We need others with which we can talk to, laugh with, listen to, and share our emotions.

The ones closest to you are the ones that can help you through difficult times. Even when you feel you can do it alone, it helps to share your struggles with others. Every person is different, but we share some experiences that are the same. Simply talking to someone can help you realize you are not alone.

Thought Bubble

- List the top three people in your life that you feel you can trust.
- Now go talk to at least one of these people and tell them about your day. It can be through a text message, a phone call, or in person.

Day 9

Good Friends

It's important to not just have friends but to have good friends that you can trust and that you know are supportive. Good friends will help you get through the difficult times in your life, bad friends will do just the opposite.

Bad friends say bad things about you behind your back, often lie to you, judge you, are never there to support you when you need it most, hold grudges, reveal your secrets to others, and pressure you into doing things you don't want to do. You don't need bad friends in your life. They will only bring you down and bring negativity into your life.

Good friends are there for you when you need them. They support you, listen to you, show empathy and understanding, cheer you up, and celebrate your successes with you.

You need to make sure that you only have good friends in your life. This will make you feel confident about yourself and you will get the support that you need.

- Think of the friends you have. Go through the paragraph of what a rotten friend is. Then read through the paragraph of what a good friend is.
- Does your friend fall into the good or the bad list?
- If they fall into the bad list, it's time for you to make a change.

This is hard to do, but consider letting go of this friend. You can start off by spending less time with them and making sure they are not a big part of your life. Or, another option is to talk to your friend and tell them what has been bothering you about them. Maybe they spill your secrets without knowing. Make them aware of things they do that you do not appreciate. This can help them become your better friend.

Day 10

Support Your Friends

A friend's job is like a two-way street. You have to look both ways before you cross the road. What I mean by this is that if your friends support you, support them too. Being good friends with each other goes both ways. Supporting your friends will make you feel good too. If you can make them feel better or give them some helpful advice or even just a fun day, you too will feel good about life and good about helping others.

Friends are important to have because you are each other's support system. Being a good friend can simply mean taking their mind off of things they don't want to think about. It doesn't mean that you have to fix their problems or that you can always make them feel better. It means that they know you are there for them and can help them if they need it.

Friends can simply be there just to make funny faces or a silly joke or two with you. We all need friends like this.

Thought Bubble

- Think of one friend you can do something for to make their day better.
- Once you've chosen your friend, choose what you want to do to make them feel better.

It could be, for example, sending them a text or a funny meme, buying a chocolate for them, telling them a joke to make them laugh, or anything else you could think of.

Day 11

Family

Family is often the best support system there is. Families who communicate well can share the benefits of support and understanding.

I know sometimes it feels like it's hard to talk to them about difficult circumstances, but the one thing to remember is that your family loves you. Not all families are the same, and some are closer than others, but there is value in having your family as support.

Family members can sometimes annoy, say something stupid, or give useless advice, but that doesn't mean that they don't love you. Don't be too hard on your family. They usually only want what's best for you and sometimes don't understand what you are going through. However, if you communicate, that could help them understand how you're feeling.

Family can make you feel good about yourself when you share happy moments, they can build you up and say positive things about you, and when you are with family, you know you belong somewhere.

If they don't do these things, it's good to talk to them about what is bothering you and what they can do differently to support you.

Family should be there for you, and they should lift you up and support you.

Thought Bubble

- Can you think of one thing that a family member said that made you feel happy?
- Can you think of one positive thing a family member did for you that impacted you?

Go talk to one family member about something that's been bothering you.

Day 12

Supporting the Family

It's important to support your family too and to spend time with them. The only way to have a good relationship with them is to work on it. Spend quality time with them and do the activities they want to do with you. Making an effort to spend time with them will help them feel appreciated and loved.

You can show appreciation for your family by complimenting them and congratulating them when something good happens to them. When you talk to your family honestly, it often helps them to develop empathy and understanding. This can help to strengthen the family bond.

Family is just as important as friends. The challenging thing about family is you don't choose them. That's why it's extra important to build good relationships with them. When you have a healthy family relationship, this will help you in your daily life, and it will become something positive and uplifting. Even the smallest act of appreciation can help them feel loved and help you build better relationships.

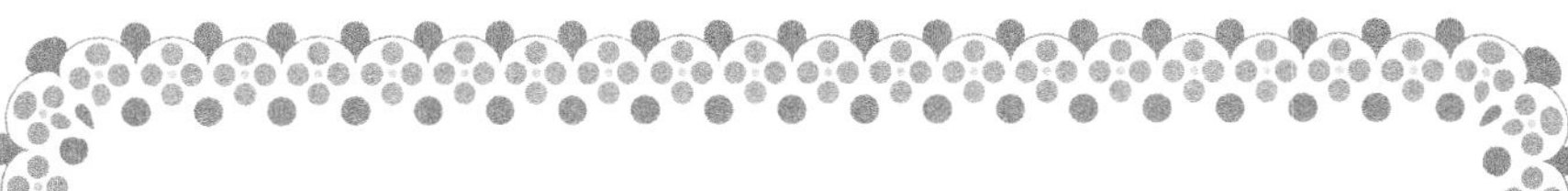

Thought Bubble

- Can you think of anything you can do with your family to bond with them?
- Write it down and choose at least one thing you can do with them today.

Day 13

Making New Friends

Making new friends can be scary and hard. But it's always good to make some new friends, especially if you feel you don't have the support you need. You can try making new friends at school, or join a club you think might be fun. You'll often find good friends at activities you like to do. For example, if you like playing sports, try a new sport at school, there will be loads of new people to meet and get to know better.

It's often hard to begin a conversation with someone new, so even a smile could help start a friendship. If you show interest, they'll notice you and might start a conversation with you. Even helping someone with something small can spark a friendship between you. People are usually friendly and do want to talk to you as well. If you start to talk to someone and they invite you to something, take the opportunity. The more events and places you go, the more likely you'll meet someone that will become your new friend.

Thought Bubble

- I challenge you to smile for at least one person today. Even just one smile can help you build up the courage to talk to someone new.
- Write your thoughts and feelings about making new friends. Think of one positive thing that will come out of making a new friend and write it down.

Day 14

Accepting Support

Friends and family are there for support, laughter, joy, and more. They make life a little lighter—If you allow them. Be open to letting people into your life and sharing your life with others. That comes with building trust along the way, but it also involves making sure your walls are down. It's often difficult to do this if someone has hurt you in the past; however, doing this will allow you to feel loved and accepted and become a little more positive in life.

If you're struggling to open up to people, you can talk to them about why you're struggling. It helps when some-one shares something personal with you. It can make you feel confident to share something personal with them.

Try to open up to the people closest to you—when you see that they won't judge you, it can become easier to do. Try to be honest with yourself and them and explain these thoughts.

The more you accept support from others, the more you will feel positive. It's often a relief to share something you've been keeping in, and the more you do it, the easier it will become.

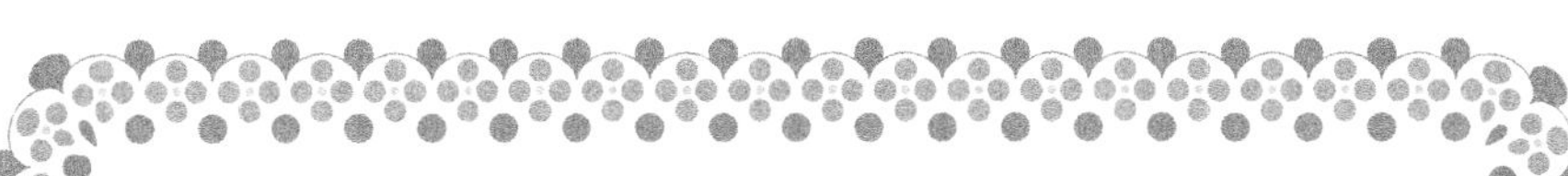

Thought Bubble

✤ *Write a thought you haven't shared and want to share. See if you can share it with at least one person you trust.*

Thank you!

Week 3
Gratitude

Day 15

It's Great to Be Grateful

For a more positive attitude, we should practice more gratitude. To get you into a positive mindset and let the bad things go, remember all the good that has already happened. Sometimes, everything looks dull and gray in our lives. But we have to remember all the moments of sunshine, happiness, and significant memories.

Remembering all the good can help us see that life is not always bad. Even if the clouds are dark and heavy with rain, there is a ray of sunshine that shines again. So remember that even if you're going through a hard time now, your ray of sunshine will shine through the hardships too.

If you are grateful, you can appreciate the little things in your life. That will help you value the good things about yourself too.

Thoughtful Bubble

- Look around you. Now write down things you see that you could appreciate more.
- Look in the mirror. Write the small things you appreciate about yourself. It could be inside and outside qualities.

Whenever you don't feel good about yourself, remember what you wrote down and remind yourself of the small things you appreciate about life. That will give you perspective on when you need to love yourself a little more.

Day 16

Appreciate the Small Things

It's easy to take things for granted in life. We forget that what we already have are gifts. Simple things like the house you live in, the food you eat, the comfy bed you sleep on, the clothes you wear, and so much more:

The sun, coming up for the day to start; a butterfly flying past you in the field; a flower blooming. We forget the small things in life easier because we know they are there.

If suddenly all the flowers in the world disappeared, we would notice how beautiful they had made the day and how dull life is without them. That would happen for everything we take for granted; We focus too much on the things happening now and we miss out on all the details in life. We should not allow our stress to cause us to forget about everything wonderful around us.

If we appreciate more things in life, we could realize that our problems are much smaller than they seem.

Thought Bubble

- Look outside your window or go for a walk in your yard and sit down for a few minutes. Just take in everything you can see, for example, any birds or insects walking around, any flowers blooming, and leaves blowing in the wind.
- Look at each of these things separately and think of what life would be like without them.
- Then think of how you can be grateful for each of these items.

Day 17

Return Kindness

Being grateful is not all about yourself; it's about being grateful for others too. Often doing something kind or being kind to someone goes a long way. Not only for you but for the person you helped too.

When someone does something kind for you, it makes you feel very appreciated, happy and loved. And when you return the kindness, someone else will receive those positive feelings, which will make you feel good also.

Have you ever shared your last piece of chocolate with someone? How did they react? Did their eyes widen in excitement? Did they savor every moment of the melting goodness? And how did you feel giving it to them and seeing them that way? It's a great feeling to help and appreciate others. You never know how much you could be affecting someone's life from one act of kindness.

Thought Bubble

- How can you show appreciation for someone else? Think about what you can do to be kind to someone.
- I challenge you to return kindness to one person who has been kind to you.

Day 18

How to Change Your Perspective

To be grateful, we have to focus on the good things in life. We should make our problems small and our positive attitudes big. We have to shift our mindset to think that we can overcome any obstacles in our way.

When you feel angry with someone for doing something you don't like, try to see it from their perspective. And the other way around too. They should try to see it from your perspective as well. It's difficult to work things out when you are caught up in your own perspective. Talking about your differences is a great way to understand how the other person is feeling.

For example, your mom asked you to do the dishes, but you didn't do it. Because of this, she doesn't allow you to go out with your friends. This makes you upset. If you look at it from her perspective, you'll see that the only thing your mom wants is to teach you to be responsible. Your mom might think that you didn't do them out of spite. But if she looks at it from your perspective, she might realize the reason was that you had a lot of homework to do. That's why it's so important to think of both sides of the situation.

Changing our perspective can often make us shift our point of view from negative to positive and help us feel more grateful.

Thought Bubble

- *Whenever you are feeling negative, try to take your focus off it and think of one positive thing in your life. Focus on this positive thing to calm down.*
- *When you are focusing on one negative thing, zoom out. Ask yourself the following questions: Can I do anything about it? If so, what can I do about the situation? What steps should I take to change it?*

Doing this helps you find practical ways to change a stressful situation into something more manageable. If you can't do anything about it, try to let it go. I know it is difficult to sometimes, but telling yourself that it cannot be changed is the first step.

Day 19

How to Practice Being Grateful

Think of being grateful as a skill. To get a skill and become good at it, you practice. Just like when you learn how to swim or ride a bicycle, you can learn how to be grateful. If you take a bit of time each day to practice being grateful, you will get used to it, and it will become easier to do.

Creating positive habits is a good way to learn how to be grateful. Changing bad routines in your day can help you practice gratefulness more. Let's think of our morning routines. What do you usually do in the morning before going to school? Do you eat a proper meal? Do you spend time on yourself and get ready to feel good for the day?

Thoughtful Bubble

- I challenge you to add the following to your morning routine. Before climbing out of bed, take away all your distractions and think about things you can be grateful for. It could be anything. You could be grateful just to wake up every morning and see the sun shining. Or just for the tasty breakfast, you are going to eat. Write down different ideas.

Day 20

Notice Gratitude From Others

To practice gratitude, we should also notice when something good happens in our day that we can be grateful for in our life. The more things you realize you can be thankful for, the more positive things you will notice in your life. How can we recognize situations we can be grateful for? And how do we notice when we should have gratitude for the surrounding people in our lives?

A kind action that someone does can be an obvious sign of gratefulness. Anything that makes you feel happy and content can be something to be grateful for too. If you had a pleasant conversation with someone, if you walked past a person and they smiled at you, the list could go on and on. When we pay attention to all the good things around us, we will instantly feel more grateful and positive.

- Can you think of something that happened today between you and someone else that you can be grateful for?
- Even a 'hello' can brighten someone's day. Think of what you can do to make others feel grateful and show your gratitude for them.

Day 21

Why Gratitude?

Remember: To become a more positive person and someone who enjoys life, you don't have to make big changes.

Every minor change you make can help you become the positive and happy person you want to be. If we try to make too many big changes in our life, it can be exhausting and frustrating. That's why you need to do simple and quick tasks to help get your mind on track.

Gratitude is something easily forgotten about by many people, but it's also easy to remember. It's one of the simplest things to think about, and it will take you less than a minute to do. Once you practice gratitude in your life, you can celebrate this minor success and be thankful for it. So let's be grateful today. Even if you had the worst day in your entire life, there would still be at least one thing you could be grateful for at that moment. You just have to remember to acknowledge it.

Thought Bubble

- I want you to think about being grateful. What would it mean to you if you could appreciate things more? Write this down.
- Think about how you are going to incorporate gratefulness into your day. You could, for example, set a reminder just to remember to practice gratefulness. You can even put a poster on your wall to remind yourself to be grateful. Think of one thing you can use to remind yourself and try to make a habit of using it.

____

____

____

____

____

____

____

Week 4
Anxiety and Stress

Day 22

What is Anxiety?

Anxiety and stress are very common within this busy world we live in. We are constantly under pressure from many things in our lives, and the chaos of the world doesn't help with any of it. If we don't control our stress, it could feel like we're standing in a small room while the walls keep getting closer to us. But don't worry, I will help you break through those walls.

Anxiety is an emotion we feel. Just like feeling happy or sad, we can easily feel anxious. It is a normal feeling we all experience. However, it can become a problem if it spirals out of control.

When you feel anxious, you are tense and worried. Your heart might beat quicker, your palms can become sweaty, and your breathing might be louder. You often feel overwhelmed about something and like you can't control the situation. When you stress about things, you feel anxious. But when that stressor is gone, and you still have that feeling, it becomes anxiety.

It's important to understand what anxiety is so that you can overcome this obstacle to be happier and more positive. But fear not, there is help available for those struggling with this, and you are not alone.

Thought Bubble

- *Have you felt anxious before? Think of a situation where you felt anxious but overcame this emotion. What did you do to overcome it?*

Day 23

How to Manage Anxiety

The one thing you should remember is that you are in control of your life. You are the one at the steering wheel. Even though you feel like everything is spiraling out of control, you can get back on track. And when there are situations that are out of your control, let the steering wheel go and only control what you can.

When you're feeling anxious, stop what you are doing and just breathe. Even if you have to finish something by a certain time, stop and calm yourself down. Think of you and your mental health and try to forget about the things that are making you anxious.

You can also take a proper break to reset and relax. Think of eating something, drinking water, or just lying down for a minute. When we feel anxious, we often forget about our own needs. Think about what you need at the moment and do something about it.

Do something completely different and fun to forget about your anxiety. It doesn't have to take long. Doing some exercise, like running around the block, can clear your mind also. Even just getting some fresh air outside can help.

Thought Bubble

When you're anxious, it's good to recognize the emotions you are feeling.

- Ask yourself the following questions. Why am I feeling this way? Can I do anything about it?
- Do one thing to get your mind off of your anxiety. Something that can help you refocus: exercising, talking to a friend, eating something, or any other simple thing.
- If you feel like you don't have time to do anything big, stop what you are doing: Take one deep breath and force yourself to smile or think of something funny. Humor often helps too.

Day 24

What is Stress?

Stress can occur when you feel pressured, nervous about something, frustrated, or when you don't know what to do about a situation. Stress makes our body feel tense, and it makes us feel shaky.

Stress can be good, but only if it is for a short time. It can motivate us to push forward. However, it becomes bad when you feel it for too long. Any external factors can make you feel stressed: such as tight deadlines, too many things to do at once, unhappiness with a family member, and more.

But once again, we can overcome these feelings. There are ways to help cope with your stress and become more optimistic.

Thought Bubble

- *Can you think of a time when your stress was overwhelming? What did you do to overcome this? Write it down.*

Day 25

How to Manage Stress

When you feel stressed, you often think that you don't have enough time to do everything you have to do. Therefore, to lessen your stress, you need to manage your time effectively. The best way to do this is by making a list of all the things you want to get done. Then, you categorize them from the most important to the least important. You can also break down this list and add smaller tasks to each item to help you get your chores done. Tick them off when you complete them. This will help you feel more productive as you go along.

Make sure you have realistic expectations for yourself. Do everything to the best of your ability, but tell yourself that you're not perfect. When you have unrealistic expectations, you won't get anything done. Don't be too hard on yourself if you don't do everything perfectly.

- Think of one thing that's making you stressed.
- Now write ways to eliminate your stress such as completing the tasks you have to finish.
- Tick each one off as you reach them.

Day 26

What to Do When You Feel Overwhelmed

When you feel overwhelmed, it can easily change into anxiety and stress and it can make you feel negative and panicked. But there are ways to help you get rid of this feeling. There's always a positive light in the darkness. A path through the chaos will always be there, and you are never alone.

If you feel that there's something in your day you don't want to do, and it is overwhelming you, create some boundaries for yourself. You are allowed to say no. Replace this with something that makes you happy. If it's something you have to do, allow yourself to breathe and relax before doing it. Sometimes, when you don't want to do something, it may turn out more positive than you expect. But also know that you shouldn't feel forced to do that, and you can say no.

When you feel overwhelmed, you often have too many things to do and think about them all at once. If this happens, take a step back and focus only on one thing at a time. Work on that thing in small, tiny parts until you get it done. Then focus on the next thing. With a zoomed perspective, you can focus on one thing at a time, without feeling overwhelmed about all the other things you have to do.

It can also help to talk out your frustrations and why you are feeling so overwhelmed. Venting to a friend or family member can help you refocus.

Thought Bubble

- *Write what is making you feel overwhelmed.*
- *Then choose one thing on that list you can work on.*
- *Focus only on that and work on it in smaller parts.*
- *Celebrate once you complete it.*

____

____

____

____

____

____

Day 27

How to Relax

When you stress and feel anxious, relaxing for a few minutes will often make you feel better. The goal of relaxing is not to procrastinate and shove the things you have to do to the side. The goal is to refresh your mind and get ready for a more productive session. It's there to help you feel more productive and positive when you start again.

To relax, you can get some fresh air outside and take some deep breaths. Or you could put on some relaxing music, take a hot bubble bath, write some feelings and thoughts in a journal, or talk to someone who can help you take your mind off things. You could do some exercises such as yoga or pilates or settle down with a steamy rich cup of hot chocolate.

Once you refresh your mind and body, it will be easier to get back to work.

- Think of ways you can relax. What can you think of that you would like to do to calm yourself down?
- If you struggle to do this, try at least one of the abovementioned ways to relax.

Day 28

You Are Not Alone

Anxiety and stress affect many people. Even when you don't think anyone will understand or are unsure of how to handle your feelings, remember you are not alone.

You can talk about it with others. It is important to get the support you need. If you feel like your anxiety and stress are to the level that it becomes too much, you can find support from loved ones or professionals. It is important to know when you cannot control it on your own. If you feel you don't know what to do and everything you try isn't helping, reach out to professionals. They can help get you back on track to a positive and healthy mindset.

A way to notice your anxiety and stress levels is to think of it as a thermometer. If your levels are low, it would be a one, up to a five. If it is high, it will be a six to a ten.

- Ask yourself how you are feeling. How are your stress and anxiety levels on a scale of one to ten?
- If you feel like a six or higher, try the relaxation methods first. If you feel like it's not working and you can't control your feelings, reach out to others for support.
- Check your anxiety and stress thermometer often to know how you are feeling.

Week 5
Happiness

Day 29

Fall in Love With Life

Being happy is a choice you make. Many things in the world can bring you down, but if you choose to be happy, you will move past those things and look on the bright side. We all struggle and go through a lot of difficult obstacles, but it's what we make of it that counts. It's what we do after the struggles. Do we dwell on it for a long time? Do we shut down happy thoughts because we feel guilty about being happy?

Everyone is allowed to be happy no matter what has happened. When you realize the joy of life is all the ups and downs, you will fall in love with life. Falling in love with life is difficult, but there are ways to turn your life into something more positive.

Being happy doesn't mean that you'll always feel happy. It means that when you are unhappy, you know that you'll eventually be happy again. You know that there will be sunshine again even when it doesn't look like it.

So how can we fall in love with our lives?

Thought Bubble

- Think of a time you were really happy in your life. Write down this memory.
- Now analyze the memory. What were you doing? What about it made you happy? Why do you think it did?

Remembering these wonderful memories can help you see that there have been fantastic times in your life.

Day 30

Smile

This might sound ridiculous and too simple to even try, but smiling more can make your life happier.

How often do we forget to smile? When we have a bad day, it feels like a crime to smile. We sometimes try to make a point by not smiling: Soaking up our unhappiness and letting it simmer for hours or even days. We use the feeling of our unhappiness to punish ourselves. But we don't have to do this.

Smiling through unhappiness can help us feel better and flip our mood into something more positive. It feels very unnatural to smile when we're down, but it can help lighten the mood. The more we smile, the more we think we're happy, and then we are really happy. It's a weird science, but it works!

You can smile and be happy again, no matter how bad the situation is. Even if you feel ridiculous, do it anyway! Any method to make you feel happier is excellent.

Thought Bubble

✣ *When you feel down, try smiling for at least ten seconds. Notice how you feel afterward. If it doesn't work, force yourself to smile again until you feel a change in your mood.*

Day 31

Find Your Passions

Anything that you are passionate about is good for your happiness. If you have something you enjoy, there is always something to look forward to every day. For example, if you love painting, finding time in your day to paint will make it so much better.

Everyone needs a passion in life. If you don't have one, you don't have something you can look forward to in your day or week. Finding something you love is very important. When you feel down, you will instantly feel better when you do the things you love. So how can you find something you are passionate about today?

The best way to find it is to look! Try new things. Search for exciting new activities you can give a go. Don't be afraid to try. If you don't try, you'll never know if you like something or not.

When you find your passion, you'll know. You will constantly think about it and want to do it as much as possible. Even thinking of doing it will get you excited. And when you do, you'll feel happy.

A passion can be anything from sports, arts and crafts, collecting items, and so much more.

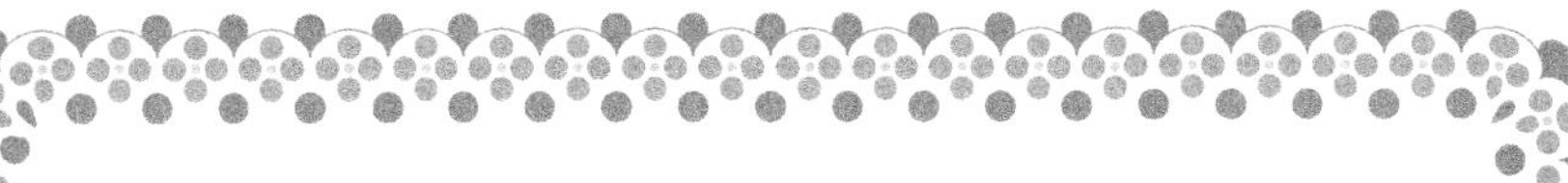

Thought Bubble

✤ Do you have something in your life that you are passionate about?

If you don't, I challenge you to try at least one new thing. If you don't like it, keep looking until you find something you love!

Day 32

Let the Past Go

If you don't feel happy, there might be issues about the past bothering you that you can't let go of. You might focus on past mistakes, thinking of scenarios that could have had a better outcome, dwelling on things you can't change. To feel happy, let all of that go.

To let the past go, you must realize that you can't change it. Don't be too hard on yourself for past mistakes. Forgive yourself for the things you have done and move on from them. If a painful thought comes into your head from the past, turn it into a more positive one. For example, if you think: I can't forgive myself for this, turn it into, it's going to take some time, but I have to forgive myself for this and let go.

Make sure not to shut your emotions out. Feel the feelings you need to feel, but don't dwell on them for too long.

Thought Bubble

- Write down the thoughts that are lingering in your mind from the past. Then fold it into a paper plane and send it away right into the dustbin.

Let these past mistakes go and forgive yourself for them.

Day 33

Look Forward to the Future

Just as we shouldn't dwell on the past, we shouldn't negatively look at the future. If all we see is negativity in front of us, overwhelming feelings of anxiety might kick in. We do not know what the future holds, and that can be a very scary thing. It is something you cannot control. But we shouldn't let it scare us, and instead should look forward to it to feel happy.

To look forward to the future, you can use a calendar and plan different fun things to do. It doesn't have to be far into the future, just a few days ahead. Another thing you can do is take a break on weekends. In that way, you always have something to look forward to doing. If you feel anxious about something in the future, you can write it down and turn it into something less scary. Tell yourself that you cannot change the future and that things happen for a reason.

You are allowed to feel nervous, but don't let it spiral out of control and become anxiety you can't handle. Instead, turn your nervous energy into excitement. Tell yourself that even though you're nervous, it's also exciting not to know what's happening in the future. So many great things can happen, and you have to wait for them to happen. In this way, you can look forward to the future instead of dreading it.

Thought Bubble

✤ *Are you nervous about something in the future? Think about how you can change this nervous energy into excited energy. Turn around the way you think about it.*

Day 34

Live in the Moment

Living in the moment helps us to live every day fully. If we dwell on the past or worry about the future, we won't have enough time to enjoy the present.

Living in the moment means thinking about the moment you have and enjoying it. If something great is happening, we should revel in it. Live it again and again and enjoy every second. Every present moment is unique. We should celebrate it and remember it as it's happening. You won't ever get the same time twice, so it's important to have fun and use the precious time you have well.

When you're in the moment, try to be mindful of the things happening. With friends and family, remember the enjoyable moments and the memories in the making.

To be in the moment, you should also be able to accept things as they are. Not everything is going to be like you want it to be, but remember that we can't control everything. If you accept the moment as it is, you will enjoy it more and gain happiness from it.

Thought Bubble

✣ *Think of the moment you have right now. What do you enjoy about it? What can you notice about this moment that is happy and good?*

Day 35

Take Risks

Part of gaining happiness is experiencing life in different ways and creating new and fun experiences. For this to happen, we need to get out of our comfort zones and take more risks in our lives. Taking risks should be something exciting and adrenaline-filled. It shouldn't give you anxiety and stress. Think of it positively. You'll be experiencing new things that will make your life exciting.

Taking risks can bring us happiness if we turn them into pleasurable experiences. When you take risks, you have the chance of not having a pleasant experience, but that's why it is called a risk. When we're prepared to take the chance it won't feel as daunting. Don't be afraid to experience failure. We can learn from every failure that happens. So taking risks is never a bad thing.

Taking that leap of faith can be an exciting adventure that can bring you happiness, joy, and a sense of achievement. It's something many people dread but is worth doing. If you are struggling with taking the leap, you can talk to others, and they can help you overcome this fear.

Happiness can come from the most unexpected places. It's how you embrace it that matters the most.

Thought Bubble

- Is there a tiny risk you can take today?
- Write one thing that excites you about it.
- See if you can try the risk.

Week 6
Success

Day 36

What is Success?

When we think about success, the first thing that comes to mind is huge achievements. You might think that getting an 80% for the test is a success, or getting a car is. And yes, they are a success, but success is much more than that. It is not only enormous achievements but small ones too. Success is when you feel accomplished after doing something and are happy with the outcome because it was something you wanted to achieve.

You can decide what it is for you. Success is moving forward and completing things successfully. You can also define it as standing up out of bed, eating, and going to school on time.

It doesn't matter how big or small something you achieve is; what matters is recognizing that it is a success. And the great thing is you can have as much success as you want. The more you succeed, and the more you recognize your success, the happier you'll get.

- Can you think of one thing you achieved today?

One achievement, no matter how big or small, equals success.

Day 37

Celebrate Any Success

We often forget to celebrate our successes and be grateful for what we have achieved, especially when working towards a goal. To achieve a big end goal, there are smaller goals that we have to reach first. These smaller goals are just as important as the big ones because all big goals are made up of them. So, if we forget about our smaller achievements, we cannot appreciate the hard work it took to reach the bigger ones.

Even if you think it's the most useless goal you've reached, every step helps towards the end goal. And if we don't celebrate these small successes, we won't have the motivation to reach the bigger ones. Therefore, being grateful for any success will put you in a positive mindset, and it will help you move forward.

Thought Bubble

- Write one goal you are trying to reach.
- Write down the smaller goals you need to achieve before reaching the big one.
- Now, every time you reach a small goal, try to appreciate this success. Tell yourself that each step is a massive step towards your big goal. You are getting there even when it doesn't seem like it.

If you didn't reach this goal, you wouldn't have gotten as far as you have. Keep reminding yourself of the minor successes you reach.

____

____

____

____

____

____

Day 38

Put in the Work

Success isn't something that just comes. To be successful, make an effort and put in the work. Get into the mindset of working hard. No one achieves the success they want by lying in bed and doing nothing. They get up, and they work!

It's not always possible to put in 100% effort, and it doesn't mean you have to do so. Doing the work means working smart, as well. Working smart is working when you feel most productive, taking effective breaks, setting goals, and not being too hard on yourself when you struggle. Have a balance between putting in the work and stepping back from it.

Everyone can do it. Even when you tell yourself you can't, you can! It's possible to achieve the success you dream of attaining.

- *How can you be productive during your day? When do you usually get the most work done? How many breaks are you taking? What are you doing during these breaks to freshen your mind? What goals have you set for yourself today?*
- *Write how you can be more productive to work hard.*

Day 39

Push Yourself

It's good to push your limits and put in the work, as long as you don't push yourself too far. This means testing yourself and seeing how far you can go. Be careful! You don't want to reach the point of feeling burnt out and hopeless. Pushing yourself can make you feel more accomplished when you achieve that success you wanted, and making an effort is required to reach your dreams.

Pushing yourself can be very good for you. You can discover what you are capable of, how far you'll go, and the mental strength you have to do it. Many people are afraid to leave their comfort zone because they think they might fail, but you need to fail to get back up stronger. It is all part of the journey of achieving success.

Thought Bubble

- *What is one thing you are afraid to do that is out of your comfort zone?*
- *I challenge you to start small and try anything that you feel is out of your comfort zone.*

When you push yourself past being uncomfortable, you'll be able to push through more tough challenges and past what you think your limits are now.

____

____

____

____

____

____

____

Day 40

Keep Going

Being persistent is the best way to achieve success. Reaching success can be a very long process. It all depends on how much time is needed to achieve what you want. Even when you feel you'll never get there, the only way to attain success is to keep moving forward. You'll have to keep going until you get there.

Every step you take is one step closer to your success. If you stop and leave it, you won't ever achieve your goal. If you continue, you'll eventually be able to achieve it. Trust the process even when it takes very long.

Never give up. You can reach success. If you feel you'll never achieve it, look at it realistically. See what small things you can do to continue working towards that success you want. Then look forward to achieving those small things because it will help you reach that big dream of yours.

Thought Bubble

- Write down what you want to achieve and what you have achieved so far.
- Write one motivational quote that you think will help to move you forward. Put this somewhere that you will see the quote and remind yourself that you can do anything you put your mind to doing.

Day 41

Improve Concentration

To improve your focus, you have to be aware of what breaks it. If there is something that usually breaks your focus, get rid of this. For example, if notifications on your phone make you stop what you're doing, then you can put the phone where you don't see it or put it on silent. In this way, you can focus on the task at hand and try to forget about the distraction. If you feel like the room you're in has too many distractions, you can try moving to another room.

We often lose concentration if we feel like we don't know how to approach the thing we're doing. You can refocus yourself by planning what you want to do and how you're going to do it. We also lose concentration when we are tired or feel exhausted. When this happens, you haven't taken enough breaks for your mind to recharge.

Focus on calming yourself down and taking some deep breaths. You can also try to develop some keywords for yourself that will help to motivate you and put you back on track. Motivational quotes can help a lot. Things like: "You're almost there," or "You can do it," and "If you finish this now, you can take a long break afterwards." Saying these types of things will motivate you to keep going, and you'll then have something to look forward to when you finish.

Thought Bubble

✣ *Write some motivational things to say to yourself whenever you lose concentration. When you've lost your focus, use these words to pull you back where you need to be.*

Day 42

Why Succeed Anyway?

We've been talking about how to achieve success a lot, but why do you want to achieve it?

Success is a positive experience: When we succeed, we feel accomplished, happy, and excited about life. It's about that feeling you get when you succeed. Humans are competitive, so when we win at something, even if it isn't against someone else, we feel an impressive accomplishment.

Success steers our life in a positive direction. It is all a part of our life plan and what we want to have in it. We receive benefits from succeeding, such as feeling accomplished and enjoying life.

If we have a purpose for our life, we move forward and know what we want to do. If there's nothing to work towards, your life will be at a standstill, and you'll have no motivation to keep going. Success also helps us feel better about any past mistakes we made or any failures we had. When we achieve success, our failures will feel less significant and in control of our lives.

Thought Bubble

- Ask yourself: Why do you want to succeed?
- Write the answer down as motivation for success.

Week 7
The Future

Day 43

How to Be Excited About the Future

On Day 33, we looked at how it is important to be excited about the future. But how can we do that if we do not know what's in store for us?

To be excited about the future, you need to be excited about its unpredictability. Not knowing everything in life and not being able to plan everything out is a good thing. If you knew exactly how each day of your life would go, would there be anything to be excited about? If we are too controlling about the future, we will have no fun when unpredictability occurs.

Remember that you cannot control every single thing, and it's okay to let some just go with the flow. Rather than saying, "I fear the future because I don't know what will happen," say "I'm excited to see what the future holds."

You cannot dwell on things that are out of your control. When you make plans, and these plans change, tell yourself that it's okay. You should be able to have this flexibility and know that nothing planned is set in stone. Know the future you want, but make sure that this idea isn't concrete. You must leave the future to do its work and not attempt to control it.

Thought Bubble

✤ *Think about your future. Think about different exciting possibilities for the future. Write it down.*

Day 44

What Do You Want for the Future?

Even though you cannot control the future, there are still things you can do to have the future you want. There are goals you can work on for making your future exciting. If you don't like the life you're living now, you can work on it to improve your life in the future.

Also remember that when you don't like the present life you have, you know that the future can be better. If you think optimistically about it, you're already on the right path to create a bright future for yourself.

It's also important not to plan out every detail, and you should have a more broad idea of how your future might look. So, let's say you want a dream job. How are you going to get there? To begin with, you'll have to do well in school to get into college and eventually start working in the field you want. That sentence is already making me anxious. Now, backtrack to the nearest goal before the dream job and work your way towards that big future. If you start small, the future won't make you anxious or stressed, and you'll look forward to getting where you want to go.

- Think of a future you want.
- Now, think of different possibilities in this future world that are positive. Be open to changing this future. If you are happy to make changes, it will be easier to accept various possibilities for the future.

Day 45

Your Interests

Think of different things you want in life. For example, what do you want to continue in the future? Your interests can help steer your future in the direction you want.

For instance, if you are interested in writing, you can focus on this for the future and see where it leads you. Discovering your interests can help you see where you want your future to go and what you want to have in that future.

If you're uncertain about it, start with your interests and see where it can take you. You can do something you love and turn it into a job, instead of doing something you don't like only to get money. You will feel much more fulfilled in life if you follow your interests, even if it doesn't give you lots of money.

There is a difference between an interest and a passion. An interest is something you think you might like or you only like occasionally. Whereas a passion is something you can't live without and think about a lot. Interests can turn into passions. That's why it's good to explore the many interests you have to see where it takes you.

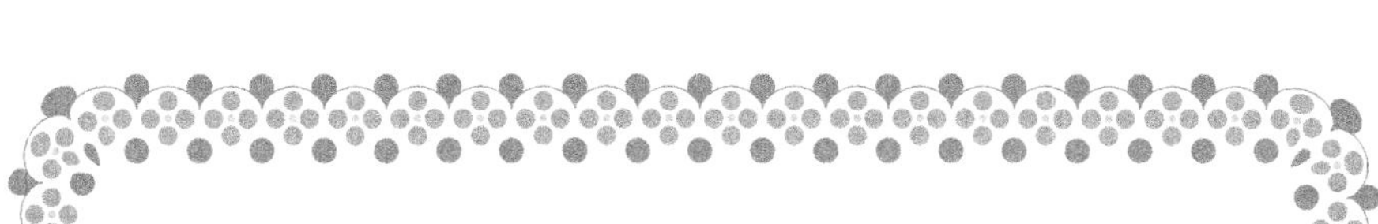

Thought Bubble

- *Write everything you like to do.*
- *Choose the ones you think you can take further.*
- *See if one turns into a passion. If you find something that excites you, continue doing it.*

Day 46

Your Dreams

To have a better idea of your future, you can think of what you dream about for it. What is something you picture yourself doing in your future? Dreams are wonderful to have because they give us hope for the future and something to look forward to experiencing.

Dreams are great, as long as you don't hold yourself to unrealistic expectations for them. However, I believe that nothing is impossible. You can reach what you want to and get to where you want to be.

To have dreams for your future, you have to know what you want for yourself. This can link to your passions and interests. What do you want to do with your interests one day? What is your dream for yourself? These are all things to think about for your future so that you can look forward to it.

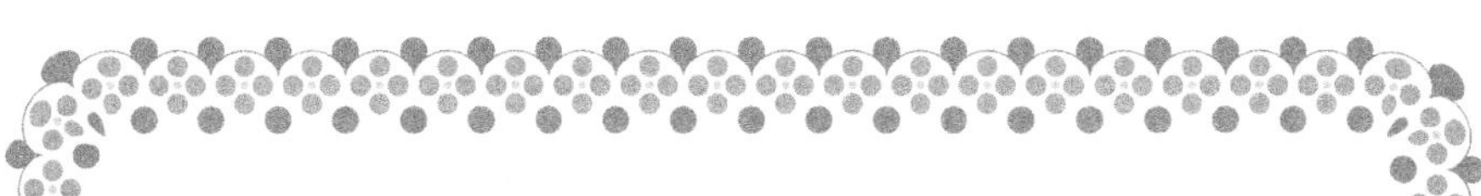

Thought Bubble

- *What are your dreams for your future?*
- *What do you look forward to the most?*
- *Name one thing you can do to make your dream a reality.*

Day 47

Expectations for Yourself

We all have expectations of who we want to be when we're older, where we want to be in our lives, and what we want to do. But we need to handle the expectations we have for ourselves. It's easy to be very hard on yourself when you're not where you want to be.

A way to handle this is to give yourself enough time to reach what you want to reach. Don't expect to be where you want to be in two minutes. Know that it is a journey to get there. When your expectations change, allow yourself to be okay with that. Things change in life, and different things can happen to change the plans you have for yourself. Make sure you know it's okay to change what you want in life. You don't have to stick to the plan you had in mind.

Love yourself and accept the changes that happen. When you place too many expectations on yourself, it will feel as if you have a large rock on your shoulders that keeps pushing you down, and there's no way to take off. Once you let go of the expectations, you will feel a sense of freedom, and that rock will fall off your shoulders. Sometimes our expectations hinder us from getting where we want to be. A different route to the same destination is not wrong.

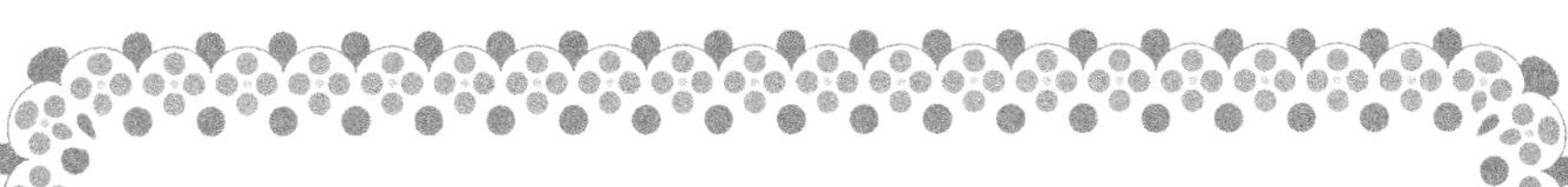

Thoughtful Bubble

- List the expectations you have for yourself.
- Look at them and choose one that you feel is weighing you down.
- Tell yourself that it is okay if you do not meet this expectation

Day 48

Expectations From Others

It's not only you that has expectations for your life. Often the people close to you, especially family, place expectations on you for your life. Maybe they want you to be a doctor or lawyer, but this is not what you want to do. Or perhaps they want you to be a certain way that you're not. It's hard to have expectations placed on you when you feel you can't reach them or do not want them.

The best way to handle this is to talk to them about it. Especially if you feel like they have unrealistic expectations for you; ultimately, parents should want you to be happy. Tell them what makes you feel happy and what doesn't. Just speaking can help your family understand more about what you need.

Be prepared to talk about the problems others have with your expectations. See if you can find solutions and compromises, but still remember that it is your life. See if you want to meet these expectations or if you have a problem with them. Make sure they know if their expectations are affecting you badly. It may be difficult to talk about. If you are struggling, you can reach out to others. Talk to your friends or someone you can trust. They can give you advice or just support you.

Thought Bubble

- *What expectations from others do you feel are weighing you down?*
- *Think about what you can do that will help you feel more positive about expectations.*

Day 49

The Future is Bright

Look at the future positively. The future is dazzling. We can either say it's dark or bright, and I prefer to choose the bright way. Even when we know there will be bad days, most will be or will have a bright side to it. It's all about your attitude.

What's next for your future is for you to choose. It's not all in your hands like we already know, but you can decide what mindset you want. Decide what you want to do when the future becomes the present, and you get to move forward.

No expectations should weigh you down. The possibilities of the future should lift you. There's a lot of things to think about for the future, like, what job you want and whether or not to have a family, but don't let that scare you. Rather, be open-minded and excited about everything that is to come.

Thought Bubble

✣ Write one positive way to think about the future.

Day 50

The Final Reflection

And so, we come to the end of our 50-day journey of discovering ways to sprinkle positivity throughout your life. There are many things to think about, but the one thing at the heart of it all is positivity.

On this last day of reflection, I want you to think about everything we have done. Have you started thinking more about some of these aspects in your daily life?

Here are some small things you can do to remind yourself of the lessons learned. What do you want to take out of each week?

- Look at self-love and how you will practice it in your daily life.
- Think of how your friends and family can help make your day brighter.
- Notice the little things to be grateful for as well.
- Recognize your anxiety and stress and how you can overcome them.
- Think of actively seeking to be happy.
- Dream about the success you want and how you want to get there.
- Think of how you can look forward to the future.

There's a lot to think about; don't worry if it hasn't all stuck in your mind. And don't stress if you haven't done all these things. You can choose what you want to use and what you do not. It's all up to you.

Having time to reflect and react can help you think clearly about your next step. Trying to work on too many of these aspects at once will leave you feeling overwhelmed, and that's the last thing we want you to feel. In your reflection, think of what you want to work on in the immediate future and stick to those. Your reflection should be a calming and positive experience to help you better your future.

Thought Bubble

- *Think about one sentence or one idea throughout these 50-day affirmations that helped you in your daily life.*
- *What helped you the most?*
- *Write anything you would like to remember about these 50 days.*

Whatever helps you the most, try to continue to use it throughout your days.

Conclusion

Congratulations! You made it through all 50 days. This is the first step to changing your life for the better. We all want to live joyful lives, but we rarely know how to do it. Hopefully, this information, affirmations, and tips will help you lead a more positive future and life. Just by picking up and reading this book, you are already making the effort to turn your life around for the better.

Our journey started with self-love in week one. Through this, we came to realize how important it is to take care of, be kind to, and just be yourself. We saw how important friends and family are in week two: how they can help to support you and how you can help to support them. We focused on gratefulness and how we can change our perspective into something positive in week three. In week four, we looked at anxiety and stress, feelings that many people struggle with daily, and how to overcome them. In week five, we looked at happiness and how you can get there. Week six, we looked at the pressures of success and how dreams can help you move toward success. Lastly, we looked at the future and how we can move forward as individuals in week seven.

The good news is that you can start the 50 days all over! If you have written in pencil, erase it all and start again. This 50-day journey will help you continue on your path of growth. Even if you do not want to start it over, I encourage you to continue the journey of growth and discovery of positivity in your life.

Remember that even if you feel like your life is miserable and you struggle with mental health, you can turn this around. You can change your life into something more positive. There is always something you can do, even when it doesn't feel like it.

Being a preteen or teenager doesn't have to be as hard as it could be. You can overcome your daily struggles. When you build a good habit of positivity now, it will help you toward success in the future. Just know that you are not alone and that many teenagers are experiencing similar struggles.

And I encourage you to be uniquely you. Fully embrace who you are and live your life the way you want. Make the most out of every moment of life, and work on yourself constantly. This book is here to help you beat stress, think positive, and grow stronger in 50 days. However, for the 50 days, it is up to you to continue your journey of positivity. Take these lessons and create a habit of them in your life. Take all the good things you have learned and go out and explore with them.

And one last thing: you are beautiful, you are strong, and you can get through anything that life puts in front of you! Go out there and take on the world!

References

ADAA. (2019). *Tips | Anxiety and Depression Association of America, ADAA*. Adaa.org. https://adaa.org/tips

Baum, I. (2016, October 24). *11 Ways To Change Your Perspective & Be More Positive ASAP*. Bustle. https://www.bustle.com/articles/182007-11-ways-to-change-your-perspective-be-more-positive-asap

Borenstein, J. (2020, February 12). *Self-Love and What It Means*. Brain & Behavior Research Foundation. https://www.bbrfoundation.org/blog/self-love-and-what-it-means

Carter, N. (2021, May 10). *Self Love and Self Care: Essential Tools for Taking Care of Yourself*. Skillshare Blog. https://www.skillshare.com/blog/self-love-and-self-care-essential-tools-for-taking-care-of-yourself-1/

Cleveland Clinic. (2014). *10 Ways To Relieve Stress & More | Cleveland Clinic*. Cleveland Clinic. https://my.clevelandclinic.org/health/articles/8133-stress-10-ways-to-ease-stress

Cocchimiglio, S. (2020). *Learning How To Open Up To People | BetterHelp*. Www.betterhelp.com. https://www.betterhelp.com/advice/how-to/learning-how-to-open-up-to-people/

Cuncic, A. (2021). *How Do You Live in the Present?* Verywell Mind. https://www.verywellmind.com/how-do-you-live-in-the-present-5204439

Donovan, J. (2016a, April 28). *Keeping in Touch With Family Can Keep You Healthy*. WebMD; WebMD. https://www.webmd.com/healthy-aging/guide/family-support

Donovan, J. (2016b, April 28). *Keeping in Touch With Family Can Keep*

You Healthy. WebMD; WebMD. https://www.webmd.com/healthy-aging/guide/family-support

Duford, C. (2016, April 29). *5 Ways to Build a Support System Among Family Members*. Intermountainhealthcare.org. https://intermountainhealthcare.org/blogs/topics/heart/2016/04/5-ways-to-build-a-support-system-among-family-members/

Edberg, H. (2019, March 4). *6 Reasons Why We Want to Achieve Success*. Positivityblog.com. https://www.positivityblog.com/6-reasons-why-we-want-to-achieve-success/

8 Mindfulness Habits You Can Practice Everyday. (2021, March 25). Projecthappiness.mykajabi.com. https://projecthappiness.mykajabi.com/blog/8-mindfulness-habits-you-can-practice-everyday?gclid=CjwKCAiAvaGRBhBlEiwAiY-yMMALMET0rNv1gweHlW61ee5stvRzVDNJV-JowYAjsCWuoeKRxjfaihoCuDIQAvD_BwE

Felman, A. (2020, January 11). *Anxiety: Overview, symptoms, causes, and treatments*. Www.medicalnewstoday.com. https://www.medicalnewstoday.com/articles/323454#what-is-anxiety

5 tips for finding things to look forward to. (2020, October 19). Health & Wellness Services. https://www.colorado.edu/health/2020/10/19/5-tips-finding-things-look-forward

Healthwise Staff. (2011). *Stress Management: Relaxing Your Mind and Body | Michigan Medicine*. Uofmhealth.org. https://www.uofmhealth.org/health-library/uz2209

Hickey, C. (2019, January 11). *The Dos and Don'ts of Being a Supportive Friend*. MyTherapyNYC - Counseling & Wellness. https://mytherapynyc.com/being-a-supportive-friend/

Ishak, R. (2016, August 24). *13 Ways To Be Optimistic About Your Future, No Matter What*. Bustle. https://www.bustle.com/articles/174097-13-ways-to-be-optimistic-about-your-future-no-matter-what

kseaton. (2017, May 10). *8 Simple Ways to Be Successful—from 8 Inspiring Leaders*. CareerZot. https://ce.uci.edu/careerzot/8-simple-ways-successful-8-inspiring-leaders/

Lindberg, S. (2018, August 31). *How to Let Go: 12 Tips for Letting Go of the Past*. Healthline. https://www.healthline.com/health/how-to-let-go#Tips-for-letting-go

MasterClass Staff. (2021, November 2). *How to Take Risks: 5 Tips for Smarter Risk-Taking*. https://www.masterclass.com/articles/how-to-take-risks#3-benefits-of-taking-risks

MedlinePlus. (2020, October 8). *Stress and your health: MedlinePlus Medical Encyclopedia*. Medlineplus.gov. https://medlineplus.gov/ency/article/003211.htm#:~:text=Stress%20is%20a%20feeling%20of

Meleen, M. (2018). *Characteristics of a Bad Friend*. LoveToKnow; LoveToKnow Corp. https://teens.lovetoknow.com/Characteristics_of_a_Bad_Friend

Mental Health First Aid USA. (2021, March 17). *How to Take Care of Yourself When You're Feeling Overwhelmed*. Mental Health First Aid. https://www.mentalhealthfirstaid.org/2021/03/how-to-take-care-of-yourself-when-youre-feeling-overwhelmed/

Nyx, J. (2014, August 12). *41 Ways to Practice Self-Love and Be Good to Yourself*. Lifehack; Lifehack. https://www.lifehack.org/articles/communication/30-ways-practice-self-love-and-good-yourself.html

Robinson, K. M. (n.d.). *How to Make New Friends*. WebMD. https://www.webmd.com/balance/features/how-to-make-new-friends

Stewart, A. R. (2017, November 17). *13 Habits of Self-Love Every Woman Should Adopt*. Healthline. https://www.healthline.com/health/13-self-love-habits-every-woman-needs-to-have

Printed in Great Britain
by Amazon

12545243R00078